Pass the Sweet Potatoes, Please!

Power to be fit healthy cooking series.

Pass the Sweet Potatoes, Please!

Velonda Thompson, Ph.D.
Edited by Jane Varner

Writers Club Press
San Jose New York Lincoln Shanghai

Writers Club Press
an imprint of iUniverse.com, Inc.

For information address:
iUniverse.com, Inc.
5220 S 16th, Ste. 200
Lincoln, NE 68512
www.iuniverse.com

Library of Congress Control Number: 20010946454

ISBN: 0-595-20228-4

Printed in the United States of America

Contents

Acknowledgements

This book could not have been possible without the contributions and support of many people. I write this as a tribute first to an educational process that has allowed me to master levels of nutritional knowledge guided by wonderful institutions and mentors like H. Ira Fritz, Ph.D.–The Union Institute. This work is also a tribute to the amazing fields of human nutrition and food science, which are forever expanding through the efforts of researchers like Albert Purcell, William Walter, and Dr. Henry P. Fleming of the Department of Food Science, North Carolina State University at Raleigh (SweetPotato Research Group) and Walter Willett, Ph.D., M.D, Harvard University School of Public Health. I extend thanks to the communities in which I live and serve, for the many friends, clients and health professionals who have shown deep faith in my ability to acquire, analyze and present information about nutrition in a way they can understand.

Introduction

The *sweet potato* is one of the world's most unique gifts from nature. It is grown in more developing countries than any other crop. This power vegetable comes packed with vitamins, minerals, and fiber. It contains no fat and is an excellent source of complex carbohydrates, folate and beta-carotene. Health benefits such as reducing the incidence of heart attacks and preventing cancer have been attributed to the nutrients found in the *sweet potato*. A 1991 study by the Center for Science in the Public Interest (CSPI) ranked the sweet potato the number one vegetable. Deliciously versatile and a hit on the nutritional charts, the *sweet potato* can be the star vegetable for a holiday dinner, a tasty addition to breakfast or lunch, or a sweet after school or late night snack. *Pass the Sweet Potatoes, Please* is an educational resource for making this wonder root a regular part of any menu, and includes recipes for main dishes, sides, and breads. Health benefits are highlighted in the "Research Says…" chapter. I hope you enjoy this book as a contribution to the advancement of fields of nutrition and food science as well as a tool that gives you the power to be fit.

SWEET SPUD-HISTORY

The sweet potato is a fleshy root originating in South and Central America. By the time Columbus came to America in 1942, many varieties were already being grown. This new food was probably brought to Europe about 1500 from the West Indies. Between the late 1800's and early 1900's, over 100 sweet potato products were developed and patented by George Washington Carver.

A **Sweet Potato** is not a **Yam.** Yams and Sweet Potatoes are both grown underground; however, this is where the similarities end. The sweet potato, which is commercially grown in this country, is a fleshy non-tuberous root member of the genus Ipomoea Batatas family. It comes in two varieties. The most commonly seen variety has dark skin and deep orange flesh. The other variety has a light skin and beige or ivory flesh. The darker variety is sweet and most often mistaken for a YAM. The yam is a large, starchy, tuberous root belonging to the genus ioscorea family. Yams grow in tropical and subtropical countries and require 8—10 months of warm weather to mature. The yam can grow up to seven feet and can range in color from off-white to brown.

Although botanically speaking, the two are not related, the names have become entwined in this country. During the 18th century, when English settlers established their farms, the sweet potato was introduced in the United States and southern producers and shippers adopted the African name, "nyami", for this vegetable. The English version of this name, "yam", came to be used. Although the terms are commonly used interchangeably, in the U.S. yams are actually *sweet potatoes*.

MAIN DISHES

Whether you're looking for healthy, home cooked goodness, ideas, or high-fiber food, this section offers a tasty array of recipes for your eating pleasure.

SAUSAGE and SWEET POTATO STUFFING

½ POUND BULK TURKEY SAUSAGE

1 CAN (16 OZ) SWEET POTATOES IN SYRUP
    UNDRAINED

1 CUP WATER

1 BOX OF STOVE TOP CORNBREAD STUFFING
    MIX

➤ Brown sausage in large skillet on medium heat.

➤ Drain sweet potatoes, reserving syrup.

➤ Slice sweet potatoes.

➤ Add water and reserved syrup to skillet and bring to boil.

➤ Stir in stuffing mix and sweet potatoes just to moisten.

➤ Spoon into 1 ½ qt casserole dish.

➤ Bake at 350°f, covered, for 20 minutes or until thoroughly heated.

Source: Nancy Goodwin-City of Detroit Health Department

SWEET POTATO CRAB CAKES

1 POUND CRABMEAT

1 CUP MASHED SWEET POTATO

1 CUP BREAD CRUMBS

1/3 CUP CHOPPED RED ONION

½ CUP EGG SUBSTITUTE

PEANUT OIL

➢ Combine crabmeat, potato, ½ cup breadcrumbs, onion and egg substitute in medium bowl, mixing thoroughly.

➢ Form into medium patties.

➢ Coat patties with remaining bread crumbs.

➢ Cook over medium heat in peanut oil until golden brown on both sides.

SWEET POTATO TUNA BAKE

10 OUNCES (4 CUPS) SHREDDED FROZEN
    CENTER CUT SWEET POTATO

2 CUPS MOZZARELLA CHEESE

1 CUP 2% MILK

1 6-OUNCE CAN SOLID WHITE TUNA IN SPRING
    WATER

½ CUP CHOPPED GREEN ONION

½ CUP CHOPPED GREEN PEPPER

1 CUP EGG SUBSTITUTE

½ CUP REDUCED FAT SOUR CREAM

½ TEASPOON GARLIC

BLACK PEPPER

- ➤ Preheat oven to 350°F.
- ➤ In a large bowl, combine all the listed ingredients.
- ➤ Poor into lightly greased 10 inch deep pie plate.
- ➤ Bake approximately 1 hour or until golden and crusty.

CHICKEN PIE WITH A SWEET POTATO CRUST

¼ TEASPOON PUMPKIN PIE SPICE

1-24 OUNCE CAN SWEET POTATOES, DRAINED

2 TABLESPOONS MARGARINE, MELTED

2 CUPS COOKED CHICKEN BREASTS, CUBED

1 10-OUNCE CAN LOW FAT, LOW-SODIUM
      CREAM OF MUSHROOM SOUP

1 9-OUNCE PACKAGE FROZEN BROCCOLI,
      CHOPPED

NONSTICK COOKING SPRAY

GROUND PEPPER

- ➢ Combine pumpkin pie spice, sweet potatoes and margarine in a medium bowl. Blend until smooth.
- ➢ Spray 9-inch pie pan with nonstick cooking spray.
- ➢ Line pie pan with potato mixture to form a pie shell and set aside.
- ➢ Combine chicken, soup, broccoli and pepper in medium bowl.
- ➢ Pour chicken mixture into prepared pie pan.
- ➢ Bake for approximately 50 minutes at 350° F.

ROASTED CORNISH HEN and SWEET POTATOES

2 CORNISH HENS (1 ½—2 LBS. EACH)

½ CUP OLIVE OIL

2 TABLESPOONS LEMON JUICE

4 TEASPOONS MINCED GARLIC

4 LARGE SWEET POTATOES CUT INTO
        QUARTERS

GROUND BLACK PEPPER

- ➤ Preheat oven to 375°F.
- ➤ Place cornish hens on rack in large roasting pan, breast down.
- ➤ Combine oil, juice and garlic in small bowl.
- ➤ Brush oil mixture over hens.
- ➤ Bake hens 30 minutes.
- ➤ Turn hens breast up, and add sweet potato to roasting pan.
- ➤ Brush hen and potatoes with remaining oil mixture.
- ➤ Bake approximately 45 minutes or until potatoes are tender.
- ➤ Baste with pan juices every 15 minutes.

CHICKEN and SWEET POTATO SHEPHERD'S PIE

4 CUPS SWEET POTATOES, COOKED, PEELED
    AND MASHED

1-12 OUNCE CAN EVAPORATED SKIM MILK

¼ TEASPOON PEPPER

6 SLICES TURKEY BACON

2 CLOVES GARLIC, MINCED

1 CUP SLICED BUTTON MUSHROOMS

1 CUP FROZEN SMALL WHITE ONIONS,
    THAWED

¼ CUP ALL-PURPOSE FLOUR

1-14 ½ OUNCE CAN FAT-FREE CHICKEN BROTH

1 TEASPOON CUMIN

¼ TEASPOON NUTMEG

¼ TEASPOON DIJON MUSTARD

1 TEASPOON LOW SODIUM SOY SAUCE

1 ¼ POUND BONELESS, SKINLESS CHICKEN
    BREASTS, COOKED AND DICED

3 CUPS FROZEN MIXED VEGETABLES

➢ Preheat oven to 350° F.

➢ In a bowl, combine mashed sweet potatoes, 1/3 cup evaporated skim milk, salt and pepper. Stir to combine. Set aside.

➢ In a large skillet over medium-high heat, cook bacon 4 to 5 minutes or until crisp, turning at least once.

➢ Remove bacon from skillet and drain on paper towels. Discard all but 1 teaspoon of fat from the pan.

➢ Add garlic, mushrooms and white onions and cook over medium-high heat 4 to 5 minutes, stirring occasionally, until onions begin to brown slightly and mushrooms have softened.

➢ Sprinkle flour over mushroom mixture and cook, stirring 1 minute.

➢ Slowly add remaining evaporated skim milk, stirring constantly to avoid lumps.

➢ Add chicken broth, cumin and nutmeg. Bring to a gentle boil and cook until slightly thickened, about 1 to 2 minutes.

➢ Remove skillet from heat and stir in mustard and soy sauce. Set aside.

➢ Crumble bacon into a bowl.

➢ Add chicken, mixed vegetables and sauce mixture. Stir until wee mixed.

➢ Pour into a 13 x 9-inch baking dish.

➢ Spread the sweet potato mixture evenly over the top of the dish to cover.

➢ Bake 25 to 35 minutes or until thoroughly warmed.

Recipe courtesy of   the North Carolina SweetPotato Commission

SOUPS

As a partner to a sandwich or salad, or a star for a meal, the soups that follow are hearty and rich in vitamins

SPICY SWEET POTATO SOUP

2 TABLESPOONS UNSALTED BUTTER
½ CUP FINELY CHOPPED ONION
1 JALAPENO PEPPER, SEEDED AND MINCED
6 CUPS CHICKEN STOCK
1 POUND SWEET POTATOES, PEELED AND CUT
      INTO CHUNKS
½ TEASPOON NUTMEG
½ CUP HEAVY CREAM
PEPPER

GARNISH: DICED GREEN, YELLOW, AND RED BELL
PEPPERS

➢ In a saucepan, melt butter and cook onions and jalapeno
pepper until tender (about 2 –3 minutes).

➢ Add chicken stock and sweet potatoes and cook until tender
(about 30 minutes).

➢ Puree the soup in a blender to desired consistency.

➢ Add additional stock or water if thinner soup is preferred.

➢ Add nutmeg and heavy cream.

➤   Season to taste with pepper.

➤   Serve hot with bell pepper garnish.

Source: The Louisiana Sweet Potato Commission

TURKEY, CORN & SWEET POTATO SOUP

½ CUP CHOPPED ONION

1 SMALL JALAPENO PEPPER, MINCED

1 TEASPOON MARGARINE

5 CUPS TURKEY BROTH OR REDUCED-SODIUM
    CHICKEN BOUILLON

1 ½ POUNDS SWEET POTATOES, PEELED AND
    CUT INTO 1 ½ INCH CUBES

2 CUPS COOKED TURKEY, CUT INTO 1 ½ INCH
    CUBES

1 ½ CUPS FROZEN CORN

➤ In 5-quart saucepan, over medium-high heat, sauté onion and pepper in margarine 5 minutes or until onion is translucent.

➤ Add broth, potatoes, turkey and salt; bring to boil. Reduce heat to low, cover and simmer 20 to 25 minutes or until potatoes are tender.

➤ Stir in corn. Increase heat to medium and cook 5 to 6 minutes.

Recipe courtesy of the National Turkey Federation

SWEET POTATO AND TOMATO SOUP

1 CUP FINELY CHOPPED ONION

1 STALK CELERY, FINELY CHOPPED

1 CARROT, PEELED AND FINELY CHOPPED

2 SWEET POTATOES, PEELED AND DICED

1 16-OUNCE CAN NO-SALT-ADDED STEWED
TOMATOES

1 TEASPOON SUGAR

¼ TEASPOON NUTMEG

PEPPER TO TASTE

CHOPPED PARSLEY (FOR GARNISH)

➢ Saute the onion and celery until the celery is softened, about 10 to 15 minutes.

➢ Add the carrot and potatoes and saute for 10 more minutes.

➢ Add the tomatoes and 1 to 2 cups water or broth and bring to a boil.

➢ Lower heat, cover and cook until potatoes are tender, about 30 to 35 minutes.

➢ Puree about 2 cups of the soup. Add sugar and nutmeg and continue cooking 5 minutes longer.

➢ Taste and adjust seasonings. Garnish with parsley, as desired.

➢ Serve with a crusty bread.

SWEET POTATO CORN SOUP

1 CUP ONIONS, CHOPPED

2 CLOVES GARLIC, MINCED

1 GREEN CHILI, MINCED

3 CUPS VEGETABLE STOCK

2 TEASPOONS GROUND CUMIN

2 CUPS CUBED SWEET POTATOES

½ RED BELL PEPPER

3 CUPS FRESH OR FROZEN CORN KERNELS

PEPPER TO TASTE

➤ In a soup pot simmer the stock, onions, garlic, and chili for about 10 minutes.

➤ Add the cumin and sweet potatoes and simmer for another 10 minutes, or until the sweet potatoes are soft.

➤ Add the corn and red bell pepper and simmer for another 10 minutes.

➤ Using a hand held blender pour pot contents in a blender and blend for one minute.

➤ Season with pepper and extra chili to taste.

FUSION SPICED SWEET POTATO SOUP

2 TABLESPOONS BUTTER

2 TABLESPOONS FINELY GRATED FRESH
GINGER

3 STALKS CELERY, FINELY CHOPPED (about 1
cup)

1 LARGE ONION, FINELY CHOPPED (about 2 cups)

1 TABLESPOON CURRY POWDER

½ TEASPOON CINNAMON

¼ TEASPOON CAYENNE PEPPER

1/8 TEASPOON NUTMEG

2 ½ POUNDS SWEET POTATOES, PEELED AND
CUT INTO ½ INCH CUBES

6 CUPS REDUCED SODIUM CHICKEN BROTH

½ TEASPOON DRIED THYME

1 SMALL BAY LEAF

½ TEASPOON. PEPPER

½ CUP MILK

SOUR CREAM FOR GARNISH (OPTIONAL)

CHOPPED ROASTED PEANUTS FOR GARNISH

➢ In a large pot over medium heat, melt butter.

➢ Add ginger, celery and onion; cook 5 to 7 minutes until soft.

➢ Add curry powder, cinnamon, cayenne and nutmeg. Cook 1 minute, stirring constantly.

➢ Add sweet potatoes, broth, thyme, bay leaf, and pepper.

➢ Increase heat to high and bring to a boil.

➢ Lower heat to medium and simmer 25 minutes or until potatoes are soft and cooked through.

➢ Transfer soup in batches to a blender or food processor and puree.

➢ Thin soup with milk.

➢ Garnish with a dollop of sour cream and chopped peanuts.

Recipe courtesy of the North Carolina SweetPotato Commission

SALADS

Salads are ideal for health-minded and weight-conscious people. Looking for a change from the traditional salad? This section offers great ideas for serving salads as a main dish or a side dish.

SWEET POTATO and APPLE SALAD

2 POUNDS SWEET POTATOES

¼ CUP WHITE WINE VINEGAR

2 TABLESPOONS WATER

2 TABLESPOONS OIL

2 TEASPOONS LEMON JUICE

½ TEASPOON PEPPER

2 CLOVES GARLIC, MINCED

3 UNPEELED RED COOKING APPLES, EACH CORED AND CUT INTO 16 WEDGES

6 CUPS TIGHTLY PACKED FRESH SPINACH LEAVES

➢ Cook sweet potatoes in boiling water until tender; let cool and peel.

➢ Cut sweet potatoes into ¼ thick slices.

➢ Arrange sweet potatoes in a large, shallow dish, overlapping slices.

➢ Combine next 7 ingredients in a small jar.

➢ Cover the jar tightly and shake vigorously.

➢ Pour over sweet potatoes.

➢ Cover sweet potatoes and let stand for 1 hour.

- ➢ Drain sweet potatoes, reserving vinaigrette.
- ➢ Toss apples with ½ of the reserved vinaigrette.
- ➢ Arrange 6 sweet potato slices and 6 apple wedges on each of 8 spinach-lined plates.
- ➢ Drizzle with remaining vinaigrette.

Recipe courtesy of the North Carolina SweetPotato Commission

CURRY HAM-SWEET POTATO SALAD

3 MEDIUM SIZED SWEET POTATOES
1-15 ½ OUNCE CAN PINEAPPLE CHUNKS
2 CUPS DICED COOKED HAM
1 SMALL ONION, MINCED
1 BELL PEPPER, CHOPPED
½ CUP REDUCED FAT OR FAT FREE
      MAYONNAISE
1 TEASPOON CURRY POWDER
¼ TEASPOON PAPRIKA
LETTUCE LEAVES
½ CUP SLIVERED ALMONDS, TOASTED

- Cook sweet potatoes in boiling water until tender (20-25 minutes).
- Drain, let cool to touch, peel and cut into ½ inch cubes.
- Drain pineapple chunks, reserving 2 tablespoons of juice.
- Combine pineapple, ham, onion, and green pepper.
- Fold into potato cubes.

➢ Combine mayonnaise, reserved pineapple juice, curry powder and paprika. Mix well.

➢ Line a large salad bowl with lettuce leaves.

➢ Place salad mixture over lettuce leaves.

➢ Top with mayonnaise mixture.

➢ Sprinkle with almonds, cover and chill.

Source: the Louisiana Sweet Potato Commission

TURKEY AND SWEET POTATO SALAD

¾ POUND HONEY-ROASTED DELI TURKEY
      BREAST, CUT INTO ½ CUBES
2 POUNDS SWEET POTATOES, COOKED, PEELED
      AND CUT INTO BITE SIZE CUBES
½ CUP DRIED CRANBERRIES
¼ CUP RAISINS
¼ CUP CHOPPED WALNUTS
½ CUP LOW-FAT MAYONNAISE
1 TABLESPOON LEMON JUICE
1 TABLESPOON ORANGE JUICE
1 TEASPOON GRATED ORANGE PEEL
½ TEASPOON GRATED GINGER
¼ TEASPOON NUTMEG

- ➢ In large bowl, combine turkey, potatoes, cranberries, raisins, and walnuts.
- ➢ In small bowl, combine mayonnaise, lemon juice, orange juice, orange peel, ginger and nutmeg.

➤   Fold contents of small bowl into the turkey and potato mixture.

➤   Cover and chill for 2 hours.

Recipe courtesy of the National Turkey Federation

SWEET POTATO SALAD and CITRUS DRESSING

½ CUP FRESH ORANGE JUICE

¼ CUP FRESH LEMON JUICE

½ CUP FRESH LIME JUICE

¼ TEASPOON GINGER ROOT, MINCED

¼ TEASPOON MUSTARD, DIJON-STYLE

¼ TABLESPOON HONEY

¼ CUP EXTRA VIRGIN OLIVE OIL

¼ TEASPOON BLACK PEPPER

3 OUNCES RED ONION, THINLY SLICED

1 POUND ORANGE SEGMENTS

1 POUND MIXED SALAD GREENS

1 POUND BRIGHT HARVEST COUNTRY STYLE
    CENTER CUT, STYLE FROZEN SWEET
    POTATOES, DEFROSTED

CITRUS DRESSING

➤ Combine citrus juices and ginger.

➤ Cover and marinate sweet potatoes in refrigerator at least 6 hours.

➢ Strain ginger.
➢ Stir in mustard, honey, olive oil, salt and pepper.

SALAD

➢ Cut sweet potatoes into julienned slice.
➢ Arrange ¼ ounce greens into 6 serving plates.
➢ Scatter sweet potatoes, onions and orange segments over greens.

Source: Bright Harvest Sweet Potato Company

SWEET 'N SOUR SLAW

2 CUPS RAW SWEET POTATOES, CUT IN
      JULIENNE STRIPS
¾ CUP CELERY, CUT IN JULIENNE STRIPS
¼ CUP THINLY SLICED GREEN ONIONS
2 TABLESPOONS. TOASTED SESAME SEEDS
1/8 TEASPOON COARSELY CRACKED PEPPER
¼ CUP OIL
2 TABLESPOONS. LEMON JUICE
1 TABLESPOON HONEY

➤ In bowl, cover sweet potatoes with ice water. Let stand several minutes. Then drain.

➤ In clean bowl, combine sweet potatoes with remaining ingredients.

➤ Toss to blend.

➤ Chill until ready to serve.

Recipe courtesy of the North Carolina Sweet Potato Commission

SIDES

No matter what you need—a meal opener, an evening snack, or a party food—this section will give you plenty of options.

VEGETABLE SWEET POTATO PANCAKES

1 MEDIUM SWEET POTATO, GRATED
1 MEDIUM IDAHO POTATO, GRATED
1 MEDIUM ONION, GRATED
1 SMALL ZUCCHINI, GRATED
1 TABLESPOON BASIL
¼ CUP EGG SUBSTITUTE
3 TABLESPOONS UNBLEACHED WHITE OR
      WHOLE WHEAT FLOUR
PEPPER TO TASTE
1 TABLESPOON PEANUT OIL

➢ Mix all ingredients together.
➢ Add more flour if necessary.
➢ Spoon ¼ cup batter for each pancake. Sauté in oil.
➢ Turn when brown on one side and sauté on the other side.
➢ Serve immediately.

SWEET POTATOES ROASTED
IN BRANDY SYRUP

2 ½ POUNDS. BRIGHT HARVEST CENTER CUT
    SWEET POTATOES
1 CUP DARK CORN SYRUP
½ CUP BUTTER
½ TABLESPOON BRANDY FLAVORING
½ TEASPOON GROUND GINGER
½ TEASPOON GROUND NUTMEG

- Place frozen sweet potatoes in a 20x 12x2 inch pan.
- Cover and bake at 400 degrees for 30 minutes.
- Combine remaining ingredients in heavy skillet and bring to a boil.
- Cook and stir 5 minutes.
- Pour over sweet potatoes and stir to coat..
- Return to oven and bake 20 minutes or until mixture bubbles.
- Serve hot.

Source: Bright Harvest Sweet Potato Company

ORANGE SWEET POTATOES
& PRALINE TOPPING

1 POUND BRIGHT HARVEST PARTIALLY
    DEFROSTED SWEET POTATO PATTIES

1/3 CUP FRESH ORANGE JUICE

¼ TEASPOON ORANGE ZEST, GRATED ORANGE
    RIND

1/8 CUP LIGHT RUM

¼ CUP DARK BROWN SUGAR

¼ TEASPOON GROUND GINGER

PINCH OF BLACK PEPPER

1 LARGE EGG YOLK

POTATOES:

➢ Arrange sweet potato patties in a casserole dish, overlapping slices slightly to fit single layer.

➢ Combine orange juice, zest, rum, brown sugar, seasonings and egg yolk mixing until blended.

➢ Pour evenly over patties.

TOPPING:

¼ CUP DARK BROWN SUGAR

1 CUP CHOPPED PECANS

¼ TEASPOON GROUND CINNAMON

¼ CUP MELTED BUTTER

➢ Combine brown sugar, pecans, cinnamon and butter.

➢ Mix until blended.

➢ Pour evenly over prepared patties.

➢ Bake at 350 degrees for about 1 hour or until browned & bubbling.

Source: Bright Harvest Sweet Potato Company

SWEET POTATOES WITH PINEAPPLE SALSA

2 ½ POUNDS BRIGHT HARVEST PRIME CENTER
        CUT SWEET POTATOES
SALSA:
10 OUNCES PINEAPPLE, DICED
¼ CUP 0NION, DICED
¼ TEASPOON HOT CHILE PEPPER, SEEDED AND
        MINCED
1/8 CUP PARSLEY, CHOPPED
1/2 TEASPOON FRESH LIME JUICE
½ TEASPOON CIDER VINEGAR
½ TEASPOON HONEY
1/8 CUP VEGETABLE OIL
BLACK PEPPER TO TASTE

➢   Combine salsa ingredients and stir to mix. Use at room
    temperature.
➢   Broil sweet potatoes until browned on all sides, about 15
    minutes.
➢   Spoon salsa over each serving of hot broiled potatoes.

Source: Bright Harvest Sweet Potato Company

SWEET POTATO FRUIT MEDLEY

1 8-OUNCE CAN UNSWEETENED PINEAPPLE
     TIDBITS
1 POUND BRIGHT HARVEST FROZEN PETITE
     CENTER CUT SWEET POTATOES
½ CUP ORANGE JUICE
2 CUPS SUGAR
1 TABLESPOON CORNSTARCH
¼ CUP BUTTER
½ CUP MARASCHINO CHERRIES

> Drain pineapple tidbits, reserving juice. Arrange sweet potatoes and pineapple tidbits in a 13 x 9 x 2-inch baking dish coated with cooking spray. Set aside.

> Combine reserved juice from pineapple, orange juice, sugar and cornstarch in a small saucepan; stir well. Bring to a boil over medium heat, cooking for one minute, stirring constantly.

> Remove from heat; stir in butter.

> Pour sauce over bright harvest frozen petite center cut sweet potatoes and pineapple. Arrange cherries on top.

> Bake, uncovered, at 350°f for 30 minutes or until sweet potatoes are soft and heated through.

Source: Bright Harvest Sweet Potato Company

SWEET POTATO & BLACK BEANS

¼ CUP RED BELL PEPPERS, CHOPPED

½ CUP GREEN ONIONS, TRIMMED, SLICED

¼ TABLESPOON GARLIC, MINCED

¼ TABLESPOON HOT CHILE PEPPER, MINCED

¼ CUP VEGETABLE OIL

1 POUND BRIGHT HARVEST COUNTRY STYLE
      CENTER CUTS SWEET POTATOES,
      DEFROSTED

½ QUART CANNED BLACK BEANS, DRAINED,
      RINSED

¼ CUP CILANTRO, CHOPPED

- ➤ Cook bell pepper, green onions, garlic and chile pepper in oil over medium heat about 7 minutes until softened.
- ➤ Cut sweet potatoes into 1 inch pieces. Add to vegetables; cook and stir 5 minutes.
- ➤ Add beans and cook, while stirring 5 minutes longer until sweet potatoes test tender.
- ➤ Remove from heat and stir in cilantro.
- ➤ Serve hot.

Source: Bright Harvest Sweet Potato Company

YAM DIP

1 PINT PLAIN NONFAT YOGURT
1 PACKAGE ONION SOUP MIX
½ CUP MASHED SWEET POTATOS

➤ Mix ingredients together and chill
➤ Serve with fresh vegetables

Source: the Louisiana Sweet Potato Commission

YAM CRANAPPLE DELIGHT

2 CANS (16 OZ) CANDIED YAMS, DRAINED

3 TABLESPOONS CRANAPPLE JUICE

2 TABLESPOOS MARGARINE

1 TEASPOON GROUND CINNAMON

4 TABLESPOONS BROWN SUGAR

2 MEDIUM APPLES, SLICED

2 TABLESPOONS CHOPPED PECANS

➤ Preheat oven to 350°F.

➤ Combine sweet potatoes, margarine, juice, pecans, and cinnamon in a 1-quart glass casserole dish.

➤ Sprinkle brown sugar on top.

➤ Cover and bake for 30 minutes.

➤ Uncover and place apple slices on top.

➤ Bake for ten minutes.

Source: Bruce Foods Corporation

SWEET POTATO FRIES

2 LARGE SWEET POTATOE
CANOLA COOKING SPRAY
SEASONED SALT
CINNAMON

- ➢ Preheat oven to 350°F.
- ➢ Cut sweet potatoes into strips ¼ thick and ¼ inch wide
- ➢ Spray a baking sheet with cooking spray
- ➢ Spread potato strips on baking sheet in one layer
- ➢ Lightly spray potatoes with cooking oil
- ➢ Sprinkle with seasoned salt
- ➢ Sprinkle with cinnamon
- ➢ Bake for approximately 30 minutes or until thoroughly cooked

BREADS

Freshly baked bread is one of the most appealing foods. From a loaves to mouth watering biscuits, this section has breads to suit every baker.

SWEET POTATO BREAD

½ CUP VEGETABLE OIL

2 ½ CUPS SUGAR

1 CUP EGG SUBSTITUTE

1 16 -OUNCE CAN SWEET POTATOES

½ CUP MILK

3 ½ CUPS WHEAT FLOUR

2 TEASPOONS BAKING SODA

½ TEASPOON BAKING POWER

1 TEASPOON GROUND CINNAMON

1 TEASPOON GROUND NUTMEG

2 TEASPOONS GRATED ORANGE RIND

NONFAT COOKING SPRAY

➢   Heat oven to 350°F.

➢   Spray two 9x5x3-inch loaf pans.

➢   Cream oil and sugar until fluffy in large mixing bowl. Stir
     in eggs, sweet potatoes and milk.

- ➢ Blend in flour, baking soda, baking powder, cinnamon, nutmeg, and orange rind.
- ➢ Pour into pans.
- ➢ Bake for 70 minutes or until a toothpick inserted in the center comes out clean.

SWEET POTATO BISCUITS

1 ½ CUPS MASHED SWEET POTATOES
2 TABLESPOONS BUTTER, MELTED
½ CUP EVAPORATED MILK
1 ¼ CUP SELF-RISING FLOUR
1 TEASPOON SUGAR
¼ TEASPOON GROUND CINNAMON
NONFAT COOKING SPRAY

➢ Preheat oven to 400°F.
➢ Coat a cookie sheet with cooking spray.
➢ In a large bowl, blend sweet potatoes with melted butter and evaporated milk.
➢ Mix the dry ingredients in another bowl then combine with potato mixture. Mix well.
➢ On a floured surface, roll dough out to a inch thickness and cut with a 3 inch round cutter.
➢ Place biscuits on cookie sheet about an inch apart and bake for 20–25 minutes.

Printed by permission of the American Institute for Cancer Research

SWEET POTATO BUTTERMILK CORNBREAD

1 CUP ALL-PURPOSE FLOUR

1 CUP CORNMEAL

¼ CUP SUGAR

3 TABLESPOONS BAKING POWDER

¼ CUP BUTTER

1 EGG

1 CUP BUTTERMILK

1 ½ CUPS PEELED AND GRATED SWEET POTATOES

VEGETABLE COOKING SPRAY

- ➤ Preheat oven to 425°F.
- ➤ In large bowl, combine flour, cornmeal, sugar and baking powder.
- ➤ Cut in butter until mixture is crumbly.
- ➤ In a small bowl, beat egg until frothy.
- ➤ Stir in buttermilk and sweet potatoes.
- ➤ Pour sweet potato mixture into flour mixture, stirring just until blended.
- ➤ Spray a 9 x 9 x 2-inch square baking dish with cooking spray.

➤ Pour batter into baking dish.

➤ Bake 20 minutes or until center springs back when lightly pressed with fingertip.

➤ Cook in pan on wire rack.

➤ Cut into squares and serve.

Recipe courtesy of the North Carolina SweetPotato Commission

SWEET POTATO MUFFINS WITH
ORANGE STREUSEL TOPPING

1 CUP ALL-PURPOSE FLOUR
½ TEASPOON BAKING POWDER
1 TEASPOON GROUND CINNAMON
¼ TEASPOON GROUND NUTMEG
¼ TEASPOON GROUND GINGER
1/8 TEASPOON GROUND CLOVES
½ CUP OF BROWN SUGAR
¼ CUP MOLASSES
1 EGG WHITE
2 CUPS MASHED SWEET POTATOES

- ➢ Combine flour, baking powder, cinnamon, nutmeg, ginger, and cloves in a large bowl. Set aside.
- ➢ Cream margarine, brown sugar and molasses in a separate bowl.
- ➢ Add egg white and mashed sweet potato; blend well, scraping sides as needed.
- ➢ Add to flour mixture and stir just until moistened.
- ➢ Spoon batter into muffin cups coated with cooking spray, filling ¼ full.

Sweet potato muffins with orange streusel topping continued…

ORANGE STREUSEL TOPPING:
2 TABLESPOONS ALL-PURPOSE FLOUR
¼ CUP SUGAR
½ TEASPOON CINNAMON
1 TABLESPOON MARGARINE OR BUTTER
2 TEASPOONS GRATED ORANGE PEEL

- Combine flour, sugar and cinnamon. Add margarine; cut in with a fork or pastry blender until mixture is crumbly. Stir in grated orange peel.
- Sprinkle streusel topping over batter.
- Bake at 375°f for 15 to 18 minutes or until wooden pick inserted in center comes out clean.

Adapted from original recipe provided by Bright Harvest Sweet Potato Company

MAPLE SWEET POTATO MUFFINS

1 CUP MASHED SWEET POTATOES

1 ½ CUPS ALL-PURPOSE FLOUR

¾ CUP FIRMLY PACKED BROWN SUGAR

2 TEASPOONS BAKING POWER

1 TEASPOON BAKING SODA

¾ TEASPOON GROUND CINNAMON

½ CUP EGG SUBSTITUTE

¾ CUP SALAD OIL

¼ CUP MAPLE SYRUP

½ CUP CHOPPED TAOSTED PECANS

½ CUP CURRANTS

➢ In a large bowl, combine sweet potatoes, flour, brown sugar, baking powder, baking soda and cinnamon.

➢ Add egg substitute, oil and maple syrup; blend well.

➢ Stir in pecans and currants.

➢ Line muffin pan with bake cups.

➢ Fill each cup ¾ full.

➢ Bake at 350°F for 15 minutes or until muffins spring back when lightly touched.

➢ Remove muffins from pan and serve warm.

Recipe courtesy of the North Carolina SweetPotato Commission

SWEETS & TREATS

Need a grand finale to a meal? In this section you will find an assortment of tempting creations.

SWEET POTATO POUND CAKE

1 CUP LOW-FAT MARGARINE

1 CUP SUGAR

1 CUP BROWN SUGAR

2 ½ CUPS COOKED, MASHED SWEET POTATOES

1 CUP EGG SUBSTITUTE

2 TEASPOONS VANILLA

2 CUPS WHEAT FLOUR

1 CUP WHITE FLOUR

1 TEASPOON BAKING SODA

1 TEASPOON LEMON EXTRACT

1 TEASPOON NUTMEG

1 TEASPOON CINNAMON

➢ Heat oven to 350°F.

➢ Cream margarine and sugars in a large bowl until fluffy.

➢ Add sweet potatoes, egg substitute and vanilla and beat for 2 minutes.

➢ Add the remaining ingredients and mix well.

➢ Pour batter into a nonstick loaf pan.

➢ Bake for 1 hour or until an inserted toothpick comes out clean.

Reprinted with permission of the American Diabetes Association, from the New Soul food Cookbook, by FD Gaines and R Weaver. ©1999.

SWEET POTATO PUDDING

3 CUPS MASHED SWEET POTATOES
1 CUP SUGAR
2 EGGS, BEATEN
½ STICK OF MARGARINE, MELTED
PINCH OF NUTMEG

- ➢ Preheat oven to 350°F.
- ➢ Mix all ingredients together.
- ➢ Spray a 9" x 13" pan with vegetable oil.
- ➢ Pour filling into pan.

TOPPING
1 CUP BROWN SUGAR
1/3 CUP FLOUR
1 CUP CHOPPED PECANS
1 STICK OF MARGARINE, MELTED

- ➢ Mix topping ingredients together and sprinkle over filling.
- ➢ Bake for 35–45 minutes.

Source: Glory Foods

SOUTHERN SWEET POTATO BARS

2 CUPS QUAKER® OATS, UNCOOKED

1 ½ CUPS ALL-PURPOSE FLOUR

1/8 TEASPOON GROUND RED PEPPER

½ POUND (2 STICKS) MAGARINE, SOFTENED

2/3 CUPS SUGAR

1 TEASPOON VANILLA

2 CUPS MASHED SWEET POTATOES

2 EGGS, LIGHTLY BEATEN

¾ CUP FIRMLY PACKED BROWN SUGAR

½ TEASPOON RUM EXTRACT

1 CUP CHOPPED PECANS

➢ Heat oven to 375°F.

➢ Lightly spray vegetable oil on 13 x 9 inch baking pan.

➢ In large bowl, combine oats and flour. Mix well. Remove 2/3 cup and add red pepper; set aside for filling.

➢ To remaining oat-flour mixture, add butter, sugar and vanilla; blend with electric mixer on medium speed until crumbly. Reserve one cup for topping. Press remaining mixture evenly onto bottom of prepared pan.

➢ Bake 15 minutes.

➢ In a separate bowl combine sweet potato, eggs, brown sugar, rum extract and reserved 2/3 cup oat-flour mixture. Mix well.

➢ Spread filling over warm crust.

➢ Add nuts to reserved topping mixture; mix well. Sprinkle evenly over sweet potato filling.

➢ Bake 30 minutes or until topping is light golden brown.

➢ Cool in pan on wire rack; cut into bars. Serve at room temperature.

Recipe Courtesy of The Quaker Oats Company

SWEET POTATO PIE

CRUST

1 CUP GRAHAM CRACKER CRUMBS
2/3 CUP GINGERSNAP CRUMBS
2 TABLESPOONS CANOLA OIL

- ➤ Heat oven to 350°F.
- ➤ Using fork, mix together graham cracker and gingersnap crumbs in a medium bowl.
- ➤ Add oil and blend until evenly mixed.
- ➤ Add 2 tablespoons water and blend until mixture has texture of moist meal.
- ➤ Press mixture into a 9-inch silver-colored pie plate (dark metal causes crust to brown too quickly).
- ➤ Bake 10 minutes. The crust will be slightly firm to the touch and harden as it cools.

FILING

4 –5 MEDIUM SWEET POTATOES, MASHED
½ CUP PACKED DARK BROWN SUGAR
¼ CUP MAPLE SYRUP

2 TEASPOONS GRATED ORANGE ZEST

1 TEASPOON GROUNG CINNAMON

¼ TEASPOON GRATED NUTMEG

¼ TEASPOON GROUND CLOVES

3 EGGS, PLUS 1 EGG WHITE

½ CUP EVAPORATED SKIM MILK

➢ In large bowl, combine yams with sugar, orange zest and spices, blending with a fork.

➢ Mix in eggs and egg white.

➢ Blend in milk.

➢ Pour filling into prepared crust.

➢ Bake pie in center of oven for 45 minutes, until all but center is set. The center should still be slightly soft. To prevent burning, it may be necessary to cover the edges of the pie with aluminum foil during the last 15 minutes of cooking.

➢ Cool pie completely on a rack.

Printed by permission of the American Institute for Cancer Research

SWEET POTATO CHEESECAKE

2–SIX OUNCE READY-TO-EAT GRAHAM
        CRACKER PIE CRUST

2 CUPS MASHED SWEET POTATO

2-EIGHT OUNCE PACKAGES LITE CREAM CHEESE,
AT ROOM TEMPERATURE

1 CUP SUGAR

¼ CUP BROWN SUGAR

½ CUP EGG SUBSTITUTE

2/3 CUP FAT FREE EVAPORATED MILK

½ TEASPOON GROUND CINNAMON

2 TEASPOONS VANILLA EXTRACT

¼ TEASPOON GROUND NUTMEG

2 TABLESPOONS CORNSTARCH

➤   Preheat oven to 350°F.

➤   In a large bowl, beat cream cheese and sugars until fluffy.

➤   Beat in egg substitute and milk.

➤   Add mashed sweet potato. Mix well.

➤   Add cornstarch, cinnamon, nutmeg and vanilla. Blend well.

➢ Pour into pie crusts.

➢ Bake 45 minutes to 1 hour, or until center is almost set.

➢ Remove from heat and cool at least 1 hour.

SURPRISE SWEET POTATO CANDY

2 CUPS SUGAR

½ CUP MARGARINE

1 CUP EVAPORATED MILK

½ CUP RAW GRATED SWEET POTATOES

2 CUPS SMALL MARSHMELLOWS

1 CUP GRAHAM CRACKER CRUMBS

2 TEASPOONS VANILLA

2 CUPS CHOPPED PECANS

> ➢ In large saucepan combine sugar, margarine, and milk.
> ➢ Cook over medium heat, stirring frequently until mixture boils.
> ➢ Add sweet potatoes.
> ➢ While stirring, continue to boil until mixture reaches soft ball stage (235 degrees on a candy thermometer).
> ➢ Remove from heat.
> ➢ Add marshmellows and graham cracker crumbs.

➢   Stir until marshmellows are melted and well blended.

➢   Pour into a buttered 9-inch square baking dish.

➢   Cool. Cut into squares.

Source: the Louisiana Sweet Potato Commission

RESEARCH SAYS....

OVERVIEW

According to the American Institute for Cancer Research, of all cancers worldwide, approximately 4 million cases each year are preventable by practicing healthy dietary practices. Medical experts believe upward of 30% of all cancers in the developed world could be avoided simply by following better balanced diets.

Ongoing cancer research continues to validate the relationship between nutrition and cancer. Daniel W. Nixon, MD, states in "The Cancer Recovery Eating Plan", that many macronutrients, micronutrients, and trace elements found in food can and do modify one or more of the steps in carcinogenesis.

According to the "Dietary Reference Intakes Report" by the Food and Nutrition Board of the Institute of Medicine, vitamins C and B, and beta-carotene frequently called antioxidants, all hold promise as compounds that protect against chronic disease. Table 1 lists several observational studies that have shown that antioxidants may play a role in heart disease prevention. Vitamin A, vitamin C and vitamin E are phytochemicals that have been associated with altering the carcinogenic process. A 1996 study (Jeng et al) found that supplementation with a combination of vitamins C and E boost the immune system. In 1993, Blot et al published results of their 5-year beta-carotene intervention trial that resulted in a 21% decrease in stomach cancer deaths. Results from the European Prospective Investigation of Cancer and Nutrition Study, the largest study of diet and cancer (400,000 people, 9 countries) showed that fiber was particularly important in reducing cancer of the colon and rectum.

Table 1. Observational Studies Showing Nutrient-Related Heart Disease Benefits

STUDY	FINDINGS
The Nurse Health Study	Women with the highest beta-carotene intake had a 22% lower risk for heart disease. Women who consumed the highest amounts of vitamin E had a 34% lower risk of heart disease.
The Massachusetts Elderly Cohort Study	Elderly individuals with the highest amount of beta-carotene intake had a 43% lower cardiovascular disease related death rate.
The Health Professionals Follow-up Study	Individuals who consumed high beta-carotene diets had a 29% lower risk of heart disease Individuals with high vitamin E intake had a 40% lower risk of heart disease.
The Iowa Women's Health Study	Women with high dietary vitamin E intake had a reduced risk of heart disease. Women who obtained vitamin E from supplements did not show a decreased risk of heart disease.

Source: Jarvis and Neville, 2000

WHAT DOES THE SWEET POTA-TO HAVE TO DO WITH IT?

Many professional athletes consider sweet potatoes to be one of the top high-energy foods. This is because the average sweet potato is low in cholesterol and sodium, virtually fat free, and loaded with fiber. Sweet potatoes are an excellent source of provitamin A (carotene) which is converted into vitamin A (retinol) by the body (Collins and Walter, 1982). The Louisiana Sweet Potato Commission calls the sweet potato the virtuous vegetable; one medium sweet potato provides over 1/3 of our daily vitamin C requirements. According to the North Carolina Sweet Potato Commission, it would take 23 cups of broccoli to equal the same amount of beta-carotene as one medium sweet potato.

In addition to being a great source of complex carbohydrates, sweet potatoes are an important source of vitamin B6 and potassium. They also contain significant amounts of folate. Research studies focusing on the role of folate in preventing neural tube defect suggest that the supplements taken 1 month prior to conception and continued through the first trimester of pregnancy can prevent neural tube defects (Whitney & Rolfes, 1996).Cell division and protein synthesis are critical to growing tissues and folate deficiency can impair these processes. A ½ cup serving of cooked sweet potatoes pro-vides approximately 25 micrograms of folate, which is about

14% of the recommended daily allowance. According to Albert Purcell (1971), an 8-ounce sweet potato provides nearly 1/5 of the minimum daily protein needs and a 2 ½ day supply of iron for women. Recently, the Center for Science in the Public Interest (CSPI) stated that, "The single most important dietary change for most people would be to replace fatty foods with rich complex carbohydrates—such as sweet potatoes". American consumers might just be ready for the sweet potato French fry. Agricultural Research Scientist William Walter (1988) says, "French frying the sweet potato may liberate that root vegetable from its traditional place at the holiday dinner table and put it on restaurant menus right alongside the more popular white potato".

LOOKING AHEAD:

In the 1930's, Americans consumed about 23 pounds of sweet potatoes per person per year (Walter, 1994). By 1993 per capita consumption had dropped to an all-time low of 3.9 pounds per person. The North Carolina Sweet Potato Commission reported a 1994 increase to 4.7 pounds per person, but consumption had tapered off to 4 pounds per person by 1999. Agricultural research scientists in the USDA-ARS Food Science Research unit at North Carolina State University, Raleigh,hope to change the trend by fueling interest in this nutritiously versatile vegetable with the creation of high-value frozen sweet potato products.

Buoyed by current reports and on-going research on beta-carotene, vitamin A, vitamin C, vitamin E and fiber, the sweet potato may become the anti-cancer food of the future. Figures 1–4 show comparisons of Recommended Daily Allowances and Nutrient levels in one medium sweet potato for vitamin A, vitamin C, vitamin E, and fiber.

The investigation of the sweet potato in relation to the incidence of cancers is likely to further our basic understanding of these diseases as well as provide practical guidance for eating. However, it must remembered, that no single food will provide the magic pill for disease prevention. A balanced diet is much preferred to the elusive perfect food and the sweet potato could contribute greatly to balancing a diet (Purcell, 1971).

FIGURE 1 Recommended Daily Allowance (RDA) for
Vitamin A Compared to 1 medium Sweet Potato

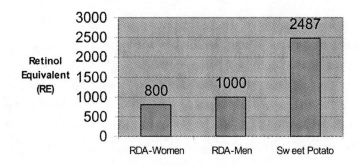

*Source: Whitney & Rolfes, 1996 and USDA Nutrient Database for Standard
Reference, 2001*

FIGURE 2 Recommended Daily Allowance (RDA) for Vitamin C Compared to 1 medium baked Sweet Potato

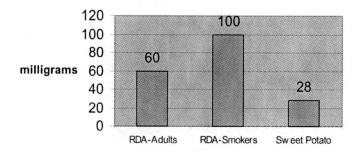

Source: Whitney & Rolfes, 1996 and USDA Nutrient Database for Standard Reference, 2001

FIGURE 3 Recommended Daily Allowance (RDA) for
Vitamin E Compared to 1 medium baked Sweet Potato

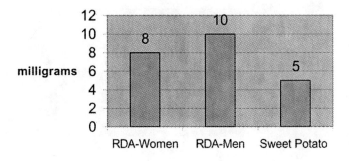

*Source: Whitney & Rolfes, 1996 and USDA Nutrient Database for Standard
Reference, 2001*

FIGURE 4 Recommended Daily Allowance (RDA) for Fiber Compared to 1 medium baked Sweet Potato

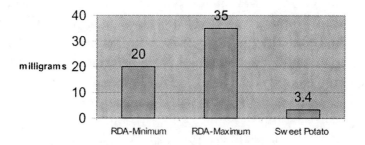

Source: Whitney & Rolfes, 1996 and USDA Nutrient Database for Standard Reference, 2001

SWEET POTATO PRODUCTS

When George Washington Carver arrived at Tuskegee Institute (formerly Tuskegee Normal and Industrial Institute) in the fall of 1896 to direct the newly organized department of agriculture, the south was very dependent on cotton. Cotton, however, had depleted the soil and threatened the region's economy. Carver provided some relief for the farmers by developing the peanut, **sweet potato,** and the soybean. He ultimately developed over 125 new products from the sweet potato, including flour vinegar, molasses, rubber, ink, and postage stamp glue. Although George Washington Carver died in 1943, extensive **sweet potato** research has continued at Tuskegee as well as the development and distribution of a variety of **sweet potato** products. Research has also guided the development of a large number of frozen sweet potato products. A few are listed in Table 2. The 1971 article "Sweet Potato: The Versatile Vegetable", by Albert Purcell, reported the use of sweet potatoes as a replacement for wheat in making bread in the U. S. and Israel and its fermentation for alcoholic beverages and various commercial solvents.

Dr. John Lee, author of "What Your Doctor May Not Tell You About Menopause," explains how manufacturers take diosgenin from the wild yam to make progesterone. From that they create progestins, the basis for birth control pills. Wild Mexican yam extract is also an important ingredient in natural progesterone crème, used to treat menopausal and PMS symptoms in women.

The plethora of products and usages for this phenomenal gift of nature is amazing. From the medical lab to the medical doctor, from the office to the kitchen, the sweet potato has become useful in many areas of life. Nature's health food is always a welcome addition to your plate, however you prepare it.

Table 2. Research directed frozen sweet potato products

PRODUCT	RESEARCHERS
Purees and Pie fillings	Turner and Danner, 1957 Hoover, 1964 Woodroof and Atkinson, 1994
Slices and pieces	Hoover and Pope 1960 Hoover 1964
Baked and stuffed	Hoover, 1957 Collins, 1978
Patties	Kimbrough and Kimbrough, 1961 Pak, 1982 Hoover et al, 1983 Silva et al, 1989
French Fries, Diced and strips	Kelly et al, 1958 Walter and Hoover, 1986 Chiang and Kao, 1989

Source: Walter and Wilson, 1992

The following sweet potato products were used in selected recipes:

Frozen, Center Cut Sweet Potatoes distributed by The Kroger Co.

Canned, Cut Sweet Potatoes in light syrup distributed by Glory Foods, Inc.

Canned, Bruce's candied yams distributed by Bruce Foods Corporation

About the Author

Velonda Thompson, PH.D. is president of Be-Fit Inc, a health promotion organization, which has provided a variety of corporate, small business, and individualized health promotion services in the Detroit metropolitan area since 1989. Corporate clients include Blue Cross Blue Shield of Michigan, the City of Detroit Recreation Department, the City of Detroit Health Department, and the Michigan Department of Community Health Promotion.

Ms. Thompson has recently completed doctoral studies in the field of nutrition and health promotion. Her doctoral internship was completed at Health Alliance Plan Senior Care Plus division of Henry Ford Health System Center for Health Promotion and Disease Prevention. The Henry Ford Health System Center for Medical Treatment Effectiveness Programs directed Ms. Thompson's dissertation project, where she served as a research fellow.

Ms. Thompson is also founder and president of Mo' Better Health Inc., a non-profit organization providing physical fitness, nutritional education and health promotion activities for youth, ages 6 years to 17 years of age.

APPENDIX A

Information Sources

American Diabetes Association
    1660 Duke street
    Alexandria, VA 22314
    1-800-232-6733
    http://store.diabetes.org

American Institute for Cancer Research
    1759 R Street, NW
    Washington, D.C. 20009
    1-800-834-8114
    www.aicr.org

Bright Harvest Sweet Potato Company
    PO Box 528

Clarksville, AR 72830

1-800-793-7440

www.brightharvest.com

Bruce Food Corporation

PO Drawer 1030

New Iberia, LA 70560

1-800-299-9082

www.brucefoods.com

Glory Foods, Inc.

901 Oak Street

Columbus, OH 43205

614-252-2042

HealthQuest: Total Wellness For Body, Mind and Spirit

200 highpoint Drive Suite 215

Chalfont, PA 18914

212-822-7935

www.healthquestmag.com

Louisiana Sweet Potato Commission
> PO Box 2550
> Baton Rouge, LA 70821-2550
> 1-800-552-4742
> *www.ldaf.state.la.us*

National Cancer Institute
> Public Inquiries Office
> Bldg 31 Room 10A03
> 31Center Drive, MSC 2580
> Bethesda, MD. 20892-2580
> 301-435-3848
> *www.nci.nih.gov*

National SweetPotato Information Center
@ Tuskegee University
> 334-727-8327
> agriculture.tusk.edu

National Turkey Federation

     1225 New York Avenue, NW Ste 400

     Washington, D.C. 20005

     202-898-0100 x232

     turkeyfed.ahoy.com

North Carolina Sweet Potato Commission

     1327 N Brightleaf Blvd

     Noble Plaza Suite H

     Smithfield, NC 27577

     www.ncsweetpotatoes.com

USDA Research Service

     Nutrient Data Laboratory

     www.nal.usda.gov/fnic

U. S. National Library of Medicine

     8600 Rockville Pike

     Bethesda, MD 20894

     www.nlm.nih.gov

The Quaker Oats Company

      PO Box 049003

      Chicago, IL 60604-9003

      1-800-367-6287

      www.quakeroatmeal.com

APPENDIX B

Selected references

Blot, W., Li J., Taylor, P., Guo W., Dawsey, S., Wang, G., Chung, S., Zheng, S., Gail, M., Li, G., Yu, Y., Liu, B., Tangrea, J., Sun, Y., Liu, F., Fraumeni, J., Zhang, Y. H., Li, B.(1993) Nutrition Intervention Trials in Linxian, China: supplementation with specific vitamin/mineral combinations, cancer incidence, and disease-specific mortality in the general population. J Natl Cancer Inst. 85(18):1483-1491.

Collins, W. W., and Walter, W. M. (1982) Potential for increasing nutritional value of sweet potatoes. In: Sweet Potato. Proceedings of the First International symposium. R. L. Villareal and T. D. Griggs, eds., AVRDC Pub No. 82-172:355-363, Hong Wen Printing Works, Taiwan, China.

Duell, P. B. (1996). Prevention of arthereosclerosis with dietary antioxidants:fact or fiction. J Nutr 124 (4 Suppl):1067S-1071S.

Garland, M. Willett, W. C., Manson, J. E., Hunter, D. J. (1993). Antioxidant micronutrients and breast cancer. J Am Coll Nutr 12(4):400-441.

Hwang, M. Y. (1999). Are you getting enough fiber? JAMA 281(21):2060.

McDermott, J. H. (2000). Antioxidant nutrients: current dietary recommendations and research update. J AM Pham Assoc 40(6):785-799.

Jarvis, J. K. and Neville, K. (2000). Antioxidant Vitamins: current and Future Directions. Nutrition Today 35(6):214-221.

Jeng, K, Yang, C., Siu, W., Tsai, Y., Liao, W., Kuo, J. (1996). Supplementation with vitamins C and E enhances cytokine production by peripheral blood mononuclear cells in healthy adults. Amer J Clin Nutr 64:960-965.

National Academy Press (2000). Dietary Reference Intakes for Vitamin C, Vitamin E, Selenium, and Carotenoids.

Nixon, D. W. (1996). The cancer recovery eating plan. Timesbooks, New York.

Purcell, A. E. (1971). Sweet potato: the versatile vegetable. North Carolina Yam Commission, Inc., Raleigh, N. C.

Purcell, A. E. (1971). Sweet potato: a sleeping giant in the space age. North Carolina Yam Commission, Inc., Raleigh, N. C.

USDA Nutrient Database for Standard Reference, (2001), Release 14.

Walter, W. M., (1988). Sweet potatoes make good French fries. Agr Res. 36:5.

Walter, W. M. and Wilson, P. W. (1992). Frozen sweetpotato products. In "Sweetpotato Technology for the 21st Century," W. A. Hill, C. K. Bonsi, and P. A. Loretan, eds., pp 400-406, Tuskegee University, AL.

Walter, W. M. (1994). Sweetpotatoes: Not just for the holidays. Agric. Res. 42:9.

Whitney, E. N. and Rolfes, S. R. (1996). Understanding Nutrition.

Willett, W. C., (1990). Nutritional Epidemiology. Oxford University Press, New York.

Index

Printed in the United States
140739LV00001B/5/A